Creative Crafts for Creative Hands

PAINT EFFECTS

CHARTWELL BOOKS
a division of Book Sales, Inc.
POST OFFICE BOX 7100
114 Northfield Avenue
Edison, NJ 08818-7100

CLB 4121
© 1995 CLB Publishing, Godalming, Surrey
Printed and bound in Proost N.V., Belgium
All rights reserved
ISBN 0-7858-0122-7

Managing Editor: Jo Finnis
Editors: Sue Wilkinson; Geraldine Christy
Jacket and prelim design: Art of Design
Typesetting: Litho Link Ltd, Welshpool, Powys
Production: Ruth Arthur; Sally Connolly; Neil Randles; Karen Staff; Jonathan Tickner; Matthew Dale
Director of Production: Gerald Hughes

Photographers
Jacket Infopress; Jacket flap Steve Tanner/Eaglemoss; Title page Infopress; 9 Dulux; 10 Elizabeth Whiting Associates; 11 Maison Marie Claire; 12(tr) Elizabeth Whiting Associates; 12(cl) Elizabeth Whiting Associates; 12 (b) Crown Paints; 13 Elizabeth Whiting Associates; 15 Crown Paints; 16 Elizabeth Whiting Associates; 17 Infopress; 18 Infopress; 19 Elizabeth Whiting Associates; 20 (r) Infopress; 20(bl) 100 Idees; 21 Elizabeth Whiting Associates; 22 Houses and Interiors; 24 (t) Elizabeth Whiting Associates; 24 (cr) Elizabeth Whiting Associates; 24 (b) Houses and Interiors; 25 Insight Picture Library/Linda Burgess; 26 Modes et Travaux; 27 Ariadne Holland; 29 Elizabeth Whiting Associates; 30 Crown Paints; 32(t) Modes et Travaux; 32(bl) Elizabeth Whiting Associates; 32(br) Anna French; 33 G Plan; 34 (t) Steve Tanner/Eaglemoss; 34 (b)Crown Paints; 36 (tl) Modes Et Travaux; 36 (tr) House Style; 36(b)Texas Homecare; 37 Boys Syndication; 38 Lars Hallen; 40 Elizabeth Whiting Associates; 41 Steve Tanner/Eaglemoss; 42 (t) Shona Wood Eaglemoss; 42 (b) Steve Tanner/Eaglemoss; 43(l) Elizabeth Whiting Associates; 43(r) Steve Tanner/Eaglemoss; 44 Steve Tanner/Eaglemoss; 45 Elizabeth Whiting Associates; 46 Elizabeth Whiting Associates; 47 Simon Page-Ritchie/Eaglemoss; 48 (t) House Style; 48 (b) Elizabeth Whiting Associates; 49 Elizabeth Whiting Associates; 50 (l) Barkers PR; 50(r) Blue Hawk Ltd; 51 Blue Hawk Ltd; 52 Robert Harding Picture Library; 53 Robert Harding Syndication/IPC Magazines; 54 Graham Rae/Eaglemoss; 54(r) Robert Harding Syndication/IPC Magazines 56 (t) Freda Parker/Eaglemoss; 56 Elizabeth Whiting Associates; 57 Boys Syndication; 58 Simon Page-Ritchie/Eaglemoss; 60(t) Steve Tanner/Eaglemoss; 60 (c) Steve Tanner/Eaglemoss; 60(b) Simon Page-Ritchie/Eaglemoss

Illustrators
10-11 Christine Hart-Davies; 15-16 Stan North; 18 Stan North; 20 Stan North; 21 Tig Sutton; 23 Tig Sutton; 23-28 John Hutchinson; 30-31 Tig Sutton; 35 Tig Sutton; 39 Tig Sutton; 43-44 Tig Sutton; 46-47 Tig Sutton; 50-52 Tig Sutton; 54-55 Tig Sutton; 59 Stan North

Creative Crafts for Creative Hands

PAINT EFFECTS

*How to make beautiful gifts and objects for the home,
from basic techniques to finishing touches.*

CHARTWELL
BOOKS, INC.

Contents

Sponging

If you feel that plain painted walls are too boring, but don't want to go to the trouble of putting up wallpaper, painting techniques known as 'broken colour work' may be the answer. These techniques include sponging, dragging and marbling. They can be used to create interesting textured effects which add a unique look to the interior of your home. These traditional techniques are fun to do, give very pleasing results and are now very much back in fashion.

Sponging is one of the most subtle of the techniques and produces a soft, mottled pattern that can make a room seem larger than plain painted walls. It is perhaps the simplest of the decorative painting effects and can be successfully carried out with standard emulsion or oil-based paint. All you need is a sea sponge and two or more toning shades of paint. You simply apply the base coat in the normal way then, when it is dry, dab the second colour on top with the sponge.

On walls that are uneven, the random use of colour created by sponging is ideal for disguising surface imperfections and irregularities; paint obtrusive pipes and radiators in the same way, and you will find they almost disappear into the background.

▲Misty blue
The cool blue sponged walls give this room a light and airy feel, emphasizing its size. The same blue eggshell paint is used on the woodwork and the walls for a very mellow effect.

Colour options

You will need at least two paints for a sponging effect. These can be either two different colours which go well together, or two shades of the same colour. Generally the lighter paint is put on first, and then one or two more colours are sponged on top.

Successful blends of different colours include blue on grey, cream on yellow, and peach on pale apricot. If you wish to use shades of the same colour, you will find that most go well together, but you should avoid picking two colours which are next to each other on the shade card, as these may be too much alike for the effect to show up.

Materials

Base paint You can use silk or matt emulsion, or simply sponge over the paint already on the walls.

Eggshell Use eggshell or its equivalent for the sponged pattern – emulsion dries too quickly and can leave a hard patchy appearance rather than the soft cloudy effect sponging should create. Dilute with white spirit if you want a more subtle effect.

Roller, **roller tray** and **brush.**

Sea sponge Choose one of a medium size with a crisp texture that will create an interesting pattern.

Rags dipped in **white spirit** to wipe off runs or splatters.

▲**Marble bathroom**
Two closely matched colours give a speckled effect like marbling.

SPONGING WALLS

1 Test run To ensure that your chosen colours work well together, test the sponging effect on a piece of lining paper before painting the walls.

2 Paint base layer Prepare the walls, filling any holes and sanding rough areas. Apply the paint for the base layer with a roller or brush and allow to dry. If the colour underneath is dark you may need to apply two or more coats. Clean the roller tray thoroughly – you will need it for the sponging.

3 Start sponging Condition the sponge by wringing out in white spirit and allow to dry. Decant a small quantity of oil-based paint into the well of the roller tray and dip the sponge lightly into it. Remove the excess by rubbing over the ridged surface of the tray, then dab at random over the wall, working from the top downwards. Try to vary the direction in which you hold your hand and the angle of the sponge and avoid overlaps, especially at corners and beside doors or windows where colour can build up.

► *Colour contrast*
The greater the contrast between the colours used for the sponging, the bolder the effect. Here strong green has been used on a pale background, showing the effect clearly.

4 Avoid runs As you work, the sponge may soak up more paint which means that you apply more to the wall, causing runs. Use kitchen paper or a cloth to dab off the excess.

5 Add another colour A second sponged colour can help to bring the effect together and mellow the contrast if it is too strong. Wait until the first sponged layer has dried, then start at the top of the wall as before. Dab the sponge lightly to overlap the areas already sponged and to fill in some of the gaps, taking care not to mask out the background colour.

tip

Sponging off
On small or narrow areas, such as door frames, it can be difficult to sponge on the paint without getting it on the surrounding area. You can get round this by painting the colour on to the wood with a brush and then using a clean sponge to *remove* some of the colour. The effect will be just as good as if you'd sponged the colour on.

Painting other surfaces

Although sponging is generally thought of as a treatment for walls, it can be carried out successfully on any surface which can be painted. These surfaces include wood, terracotta, ceramics and even plastics. Generally the only difference in the technique used for these surfaces and for walls is in the type of paint which should be used.

▼ Door ways
A sponged paint effect using eggshell in two toning colours gives a simple panelled door an attractive, marbled finish. Pick out the panelling only in a plain colour if you prefer.

SPONGING WOOD

1 Prepare the surface If the original paint is in good condition, sand smooth, but if it is flaking, strip off and apply a primer.

2 Apply base colour Apply an oil-based paint as the base colour, such as eggshell or satin-finish wood paint. Leave to dry completely.

3 Sponging Sponge on the second colour of paint in the same way as for a wall. Leave to dry and sponge on a third colour if required.

▲ Potted pleasures
Terracotta is fun to decorate with broken colour techniques. Paint plant pots to match the flowers you plant in them for a really bright and cheerful display.

◄ Diamond delight
Standard white tiles have been given a new look by applying peach eggshell paint all over. When dry, masking tape masks off the edges of the diamonds and the green is sponged on top.

SPONGING TERRACOTTA

Terracotta lamp bases, pots and jugs are fun to paint in this way because results are achieved quickly. The technique is exactly the same as for walls, with an emulsion base coat and eggshell for the sponged layers.

SPONGING TILES

There is no need for a base coat when sponging tiles. Just clean the tiles thoroughly with soap and water, leave to dry and then sponge on an eggshell colour which tones in with the original tiles. Apply a second or even a third colour of eggshell in the same way if desired.

SPONGING PLASTIC

Plastics, such as melamine kitchen units or cupboard doors, can be sponged in exactly the same way as tiles. Use either eggshell or gloss for the base coat and sponged layer.

Ragging and stippling

Broken colour-work techniques – where one colour is partially applied on top of another to create an attractive mottled effect – are popular decorating choices for walls and woodwork. They are particularly appropriate for country style decors because they have a softening effect on the base colour, which conveys the mellowness of the countryside, and provides an ideal backdrop for simple rustic furnishings.

As we have seen on pages 9–12, sponging is perhaps the easiest of the broken-colour techniques, and conse-quently one of the most frequently used. However there are other techniques which you may like to try, including ragging and stippling which are attractive alternatives to sponging, and which give slightly different effects.

Interior designers and professional decorators use these techniques to improve the feel of a room; to add light or warmth, or even to convey the impression of greater space and airiness. Yet although used by professionals, these techniques are not difficult, giving good results even to home decorators.

▲ *Country setting*
Ragged paint effects give walls an antique, rustic look which is very welcoming. Closer to (inset), the attractive, mottled appearance of the paint can be seen.

13

Achieving these effects

Two layers of paint are used for ragging or stippling – a base coat of paint, and a second layer of tinted glaze. The pale base coat is painted on first and left to dry, and then the glaze, which is a dilute colour, is applied on top with a large brush. Before the glaze has dried, a dry brush or cloth is pressed over it to make the pattern, removing some of the glaze to reveal the base coat.

Ragging A variation of sponging which creates an irregular and slightly angular effect. Instead of a sponge, a clean piece of cotton or linen, scrunched paper, chamois leather or even plastic bags are pressed into the glaze to form the pattern. Standard emulsion paints can be used for the base coat, with a thinned layer of emulsion – which has an opaque colour – on top. However, an eggshell base coat and proper glaze – which has a translucent colour – give softer, glowing results.

Stippling A second variation of sponging which creates a more subtle effect than ragging. The pattern is formed by pressing the wet glaze with a dry brush – the finer the brush, the more subtle the pattern. A proper stippling brush, available from art shops, produces such a fine effect that it adds depth rather than pattern to the finished colour. More defined results can be achieved by using a rough brush, such as a dustpan brush, a textured roller or even a cloth to press the pattern into the glaze.

Colour and effect

In general, like sponging, the best way to achieve the paint effects is to put the lighter of the two colours on to the wall first. The sharper the contrast between the two colours used, the more dramatic an effect, but for a country look pale, closely linked colours are most appropriate. Pastels over white or cream are particular favourites.

Materials

Eggshell paint for the base coat.

Transparent oil glaze for the dragged layer. Clear glaze, sometimes called scumble glaze, is available from specialist art shops. Alternatively make your own from one part linseed oil and three parts turpentine.

Tint for the glaze. Use artist's oil paints to tint a clear glaze or use thinned paint as the tinted glaze.

White spirit, a **paint brush** for paint and glaze and a **paint kettle** for mixing.

Pre-painted hardboard for trying out the technique and checking the colour mix.

For ragging: clean cloths, plastic bags, chamois leather or paper (other than newspaper where the print may come off) to make the pattern.

For stippling: a thick brush, textured roller or a cloth wrapped smoothly around a block of wood (such as a sanding block) to make a pad.

Protective clothing and **dust sheets.**

◄ **Instant warmth**
Plain white walls are given a face-lift with a warm apricot colour ragged on top with a loosely woven cloth. On close inspection (above), the grained effect, created by the cloth's weave, can be seen.

A RAGGED FINISH

1 Test run Before painting the wall, it is advisable to check that the colours you are using work well together. Apply the base coat on to hardboard or thick card, leave to dry and paint on the tinted glaze. Rag over it to check the effect.

2 Applying the base coat Prepare the wall for painting and wipe down to remove dust. Apply one or two coats of the base paint – preferably eggshell. Leave to dry.

3 Applying the glaze In a paint kettle, mix 7 parts of transparent oil glaze, to 2 parts tint and 1 part white spirit. Use an old spoon or cup to measure out each one. Place the material you are going to use for the ragging close to hand since it is necessary to rag the surface before the glaze is dry. Apply the glaze over a 50cm (½yd) strip of wall with a large, soft brush.

▲ Striped variation

Taking a cue from the wide, ragged panelling round the bath, the walls are ragged in stripes of the same width. Use masking tape and a spirit level to ensure straight edges.

5 Keeping clean Fabric cloths or bags will need to be changed when they have become saturated with glaze. If using leather, soak in white spirit before you start and clean with white spirit at intervals. Wear rubber gloves to keep your hands clean.

4 Ragging off Work over the glazed area, ragging over the paint to create an attractive effect. There are two ways of doing this: either you can scrunch the material into a ball and use it like a sponge to dab off the glaze (left); or you can mould it into a sausage shape and roll it over the glaze from top to bottom (right). These two methods give slightly different results, so experiment before you start.

6 Finishing off Continue in the same way to apply the glaze and rag off until the room is finished. If the room can't be decorated in one go, complete one wall at a time, since slight variations are less likely to show this way.

A STIPPLED FINISH

1 Preparation Prepare the wall for painting, filling and sanding as necessary, and then wipe down to remove any dust. Test your colour combination and apply the base coat of eggshell to the wall as in steps 1 and 2 on page 14. When testing the colours, first try out your chosen brush to check that it gives the sort of effect you want.

2 Stippling Mix the glaze as for a ragged effect and brush a very thin layer on the wall in a 50cm (½yd) wide strip from ceiling to floor. Starting at the top, press into the glaze with a stippling brush (top), household brush (middle) or textured roller (bottom) to make the pattern. Alternatively use a fabric pad. Keep an even pressure, but don't press too hard.

3 Completing the job Work in the same way around the room, cleaning your tools as necessary – paint-soaked cloths should be replaced at intervals, brushes wiped on rags or paper, and rollers cleaned by rolling them on paper. Try not to break off in the middle of a wall. If you are likely to need to mix up more glaze, do so before starting a wall.

tip

All change
If your existing colour scheme is either too drab or too bold, a layer of sponged, ragged or stippled glaze will transform it. Use a translucent glaze for a subtle change or thinned eggshell for dramatic results.

▲ Roughing it
A rough brush, used to stipple a yellow ochre glaze on to white walls, creates a prominent, textured pattern rather like sandstone. The plant pot on the table has also been painted with broken-colour work techniques to create a marbled effect which uses the same colours.

Dragging and combining

In addition to the random paint effects of sponging and rag rolling you can try your hand at the techniques of dragging and combing for a slightly more formal finish. The base coat should be of a non-absorbent paint such as eggshell, with a layer of glaze painted over the surface. Instead of a sponge or cloth, a rough brush or comb is dragged over the glazed layer, revealing the background colour and giving a fine or coarse striped effect. You can also produce a woven effect by applying a second layer of glaze and dragging it off horizontally. This effect is not only attractive, but helps to cover any wobbles in the first layer.

Dragging

This paint effect looks best on walls with an even finish as the straight lines will emphasize any unevenness in the sur-face. On large areas it takes practice to keep the lines straight, so you may wish to confine dragging to doors and other woodwork or opt for a woven effect.

For a soft, romantic look in bedrooms and bathrooms, pastel colours used over a white ground look attractive. In living and dining rooms a glaze in a slightly darker tone than the background colour works well.

Working in pairs

If you plan to drag the walls of a room try to find someone to work with. This will ensure a much better finish. Dragging works best while the glaze is still wet so while one person applies the glaze the other can concentrate on the dragged finish before it dries. To avoid patchi-ness do not stop until you reach a natural break, like a corner.

Combing

The effect achieved by combing is bolder and much more dramatic. Combing a whole wall would probably be too much but it can be effective used on furniture, or as a decorative feature at the level of a dado rail.

Combed patterns

Wavy lines, zigzags, fan shaped arcs and woven effects are some of the patterns you can produce using a comb. Try out your ideas on a sheet of card first before transferring them to the wall or a piece of furniture.

▼ Combed detailing
Paint effects can be mixed and matched endlessly. Here a rag rolled wall has had a combed wavy band worked across it at dado rail height.

Materials

A brush such as a **paper-hanging brush** is ideal unless you plan to do a lot of dragging in which case a proper **dragging brush** would be a worthwhile investment.

Graining combs are available at specialist paint shops, or you can make your own by cutting notches into the edge of a piece of plastic or vinyl flooring.

Eggshell paint in the base colour.

Glaze (see page 14).

A **paint kettle** or **roller tray**.

Rags to wipe off the dragging brush.

White spirit.

Step ladder.

FOR A DRAGGED FINISH

1 Preparation Prepare the surface thoroughly, filling any cracks and holes and sanding until completely smooth – any irregularities will be accentuated by the glazed finish.

2 Applying the base coat Apply one or two coats of eggshell for the base coat and leave to dry.

3 Checking the effect Test the effect by painting a piece of hardboard or thick card with the base paint and then the glaze.

4 Applying the glaze Mix the glaze as for ragging and paint an area of about 50cm (20in) wide down the wall or the panel of a door.

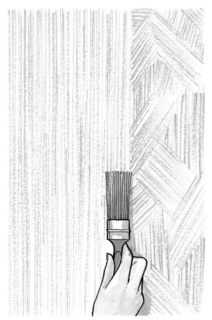

5 Dragging it off With a dry dragging brush, drag it through the glaze, working from ceiling to floor, and pressing down firmly to spread the bristles of the brush. If you are dragging a door or a piece of wooden furniture, follow the grain of the wood.

6 Keeping the work even Work smoothly in parallel lines. If the wall is too long to finish in one continuous movement from top to bottom, work down as far as possible, then work up from the bottom to meet the stripe. You may need to feather the edges where the brush strokes meet to avoid an obvious join. Try to stagger the meeting points along the wall so that you don't get a band where brush strokes join. From time to time, wipe the brush clean with a rag wrung out in white spirit to prevent a build-up of paint.

7 Completing the effect Once you have finished one section, move on to the next, applying the glaze carefully to ensure that you don't overlap the first section. Any build up of paint at the top and bottom should be feathered out with a dry brush. To avoid this in the first place, use less pressure on the brush at the start and end of each brush stroke.

▲ Go with the flow
A dragged finish looks great on this wall where it echoes the natural grain of the wood on the dresser. Here a pale yellow base coat has been glazed in a darker shade and then dragged.

8 Horizontal dragging If you wish, apply a second layer of glaze when the first is dry, and drag off horizontally to achieve a woven effect. You don't need to drag the whole width of a wall in one go since the effect is sufficiently textured to hide the joins.

▲ Cupboard love
Dragging gives a very effective and expensive-looking finish to kitchen unit doors. Even plywood doors can be painted in this way, and if you follow the direction of graining in solid wood doors, you can make the effect very convincing.

▶ Against the grain
Walls look attractive with two layers of glaze in the same colour, each dragged off in a different direction to give a woven effect like a fabric covering.

Where to start
Begin your painting in an unobtrusive part of the room — behind a door perhaps — your technique will improve with practice as you work round to more prominent areas.

FOR A COMBED EFFECT

1 Preparation Apply the background colour to the prepared surface as for dragging.

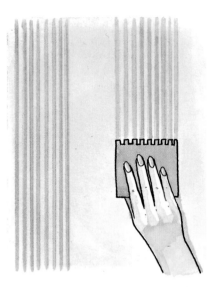

2 Combing a pattern Apply the glaze and then drag the comb through the glaze to reveal the base coat. Wipe off the excess paint on a rag to prevent re-applying the paint you have taken off.

3 Masking off If you want to limit the area to be combed, use masking tape to define the area you are working on.

▲ Combining techniques
A confident use of both dragging and combing. The walls are dragged first then equally spaced bands are combed over the dragged surface. Finally, a wavy combed edge zigzags down each band. A plumb line suspended away from the wall, or a length of wood can be used as a guide.

◄ Tray detail
Paint effects should not be confined to walls and furniture. Here a tray has been decorated using a combed effect.

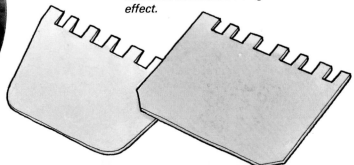

Colour washing walls

With their soft translucent colours and subtle brush-marked textures, colour-washed walls are the epitome of country cottage decoration. Essentially, the random application technique of colour washing allows a hint of a basecoat colour to appear through a wash of a weak, contrasting or complementary coloured topcoat. The overall result has a unique weathered quality that really glows.

Prior to the advent of modern paints, distemper was generally used on walls. However, it did not provide such an even, opaque covering as emulsion paints today. To overcome the shortcomings of the material and to disguise the harsh brush marks that showed up in the painting, decorators devised techniques that softened the effect and provided a textured, uneven colour finish. The result was colour washing, which has acquired a special rustic significance.

Colour washing can be used in many ways. Simple, one-colour washes provide an ideal background for other paint decorating techniques like wall stencils and borders. Exciting effects can be created using several colours as well. Painting one colour on top of another in interesting colour combinations allows the first shade to merge with or peep enticingly through the next.

This finish looks equally effective on smooth or uneven walls but is not really suitable for other surfaces. However, a similar finish called colour rubbing, sometimes also referred to as colour washing or wiping, can be applied to natural timber.

◀ **Premeditated roughness**
The apparent crude charm of the blue colour-washed wall belies the craft that goes into producing this effect. While the brushwork in the paint is still clearly visible, the original bold, random strokes have been buffed to soften the finish.

21

How to colour wash

In colour washing, thin coats of paint are brushed haphazardly in all directions over a different background colour. Sufficient pressure should be applied to leave crude brush marks that show up clearly. After the paint has been applied, and while it is still wet, a dry brush is lightly stroked over the paint to soften these brush marks. The subtle details in the colour washing develop as you manoeuvre the paint about; the roughness of the finished effect depends totally on how far you take this smoothing out process. When the paint is partially dry, it can be brushed again, but harder this time, so that more of the background colour is revealed.

Colour can be built up and changed by using a number of different coloured glazes worked over and into each other. Brush each glaze while it is still wet. Then let the glaze dry before spreading the next layer around. However, if more than three coats of glaze are used, the translucent quality, the hallmark of colour washing, is lost.

As an alternative to using a brush to remove the strokes you can also use a cloth. This gives a more mottled finish; the amount of basecoat revealed can be carefully controlled by the amount of dabbing and stroking on the wet paint.

Suitable glazes

Either diluted emulsion paint or an oil-based glaze can be used for colour washing.

An oil-based glaze is made by mixing scumble glaze, a transparent jelly-like material available from art supply shops, and eggshell paint. This is easiest to use because the thicker consistency allows you to apply thick strokes of colour without it running down the wall. Use this over a base colour of eggshell which is also oil-based.

Emulsion paint is very runny, because it needs to be watered down to provide the translucent finish that allows the colour beneath to show through and is therefore more difficult to apply. Use a ratio of about one part paint to three parts water. The best way to counteract the thinned paint's tendency to run down the wall is to enlist support. One person applies the paint and the other follows behind with the dry brush. Use water-based paint over a ground coat of emulsion.

Materials for an oil-based colour wash

Paint Eggshell paint, with its subtle sheen, is ideal or you can use white undercoat tinted with artist's oil colours which come in tubes from art shops. It is important to use an oil-based paint. Water-based paint like emulsion would be incompatible with the oil-based glaze.

Scumble glaze For the colour wash, you will need a transparent oil glaze, known as scumble glaze, to maintain the consistency of the paint while adding a translucency to the colour. This is now available from most decorating shops.

White spirit

Paint kettle

Brushes For colour washing you need two large decorating brushes, 100-150mm (4-6in) size is ideal. You can also use a lint-free cotton cloth; old white cotton sheeting works well.

Plastic sheets Colour washing can be messy as the dilute glaze may run and splash. Protect yourself and your surroundings, keeping a rag handy to wipe up any spills.

▼ **Brindled beauty** *The carefully developed brush streaks in the terracotta glaze are characteristic of colour washing. Light falling on the uneven colour of the warm, translucent glaze causes it to shimmer and glow.*

COLOUR WASHING A WALL

1 **Applying the base colour** Paint th th eggshell paint or tinted undercoat in the colo for the base coat. Allow to dry overnight. Add a s f the same colour. Again leave to dry overnigh .

2 **Mixing the glaze** Use the paint kettle to mix the glaze in a ratio of 50 per cent eggshell paint, 30 per cent scumble glaze and 20 per cent white spirit. Stir well to blend thoroughly.

3 **Applying the glaze** The more casually the glaze is applied the better the result is likely to be. Brush it on to the wall from every direction and in large criss-cross movements. The paint goes on easily.

4 **Softening brush strokes** Almost immediately remove any hard brush marks. Use a dry brush and light strokes going over the wet glaze so that obvious brush marks are softened. Wipe the brush regularly with a dry cloth. If you are happy with the finish at this stage, leave to dry. If you want more of the base colour to show through the top coat, or if you want to add a second colour, go on to Step 5.

tip

5 **Revealing more base colour** Before the paint dries go over it a second time with the dry brush. Use the brush more firmly this time so that you remove areas of glaze to reveal more of the base colour. When the glaze is dry you can apply a second colour glaze if you want to, repeating steps 3, 4 and 5.

Using a rag
Follow steps 1-3 above, then form a loose ball with a clean rag and, while the paint is wet, use a mixture of dabbing and light rubbing movements on the surface, to remove brush marks and reveal as much background colour as you desire.

Choosing colours

Try out colours first on a large sheet of lining paper. Stick it up on the wall to check the result in both day and electric light before you decorate the wall itself. In addition to conventional rural shades, experiment with exciting colour mixes and brighter colours.

Soft colours mimic country cottage walls most effectively and usually look best applied over a light background. In a cold room, create constantly sun-kissed dappled walls by using sunny yellow, coral or bright pink. Try cool under-water tones of aqua, moss green or hydrangea blue in a sunny room.

Strong colours can be very effective for the brush strokes and, because the paint is applied thinly, the colour is unlikely to be overpowering. Try a pastel base with two colours over it. Colours that harmonize are very effective: paint a pale pink wall with magenta, than add a topcoat of scarlet; experiment with emerald green over turquoise or royal blue over bright red.

To seal the finish you can add a coat of varnish; this is probably a good idea in well-used areas like kitchens. On light colours use matt or satin finish; gloss gives a rich sheen to deep colours.

► Urbane colour washing
Russet-washed walls appear quite at home even in dignified surroundings, complementing wooden boards and elegantly framed pictures.

▲ Mottled tones
The blotchiness of colour-washed walls exemplifies a timeworn rustic appearance which looks most authentic when rendered in earthy shades of green, brown and blue.

► On a cool wash
Colour washing a light aquamarine glaze behind the shelf provides a delicately textured background for a pattern of floral motifs loosely cribbed from the china on display.

tip

Avoiding disappointment
If you are dissatisfied with the colour of a newly painted wall, colour washing can correct the results. A thinned coat of a paler or deeper shade of the same colour, or even a quite different colour, can be used to improve the scheme. It only takes a little time and a small amount of paint. Improve a very strong colour by mixing some of the left over paint with white emulsion before thinning with water and brushing over the walls.

Hand painting motifs

Free-hand painting is a wonderful way of adding individual and co-ordinating touches to your home decorations without spending a great deal of time or money. You don't have to be very artistic – a playful, naive image casually applied is frequently the most attractive and successful way to create instant impact. Any minor imperfections such as smudges simply add to the charm of the decoration.

Hints for beginners
The best plan for a novice painter is to copy a striking, but simple motif from a picture or wallpaper. Traditional folk-art is an ideal starting point because the images are straightforward.

Whether you are copying designs or creating your own, always map them out on a piece of paper first. Use coloured pencils or acrylic paints to arrive at a colour scheme that will work with the room. Then use the sketch to assess where to position and paint the design on your piece of furniture.

Initially plan to paint small, clearly defined areas; a neat, compact 'canvas' like a cupboard door panel or even a chair rail is quite reassuring for the inexperienced artist. Fix your paper plan to the piece of furniture to see if the colours and scale work all right. If they do, lightly sketch the design in pencil on to the flat surface. Alternatively, you can transfer the pattern by slipping a piece of dressmaker's carbon paper behind the plan and softly tracing around the outline with a blunt pencil.

◀▼ *A painted nosegay*
Hand-painting a cheerful posy on its top rail endows this plain chair with simple charm. The motif is repeated here for you to copy.

How to paint flowers

If in doubt about your technique and capabilities at first, stick to simple examples of folk-art designs, like barge painting. Here the motifs are built up with a basic petal-shaped stroke which is not difficult to master.

In your mind's eye, reduce the flower to its simplest outline. For many, like daisies, buttercups, poppies and roses, this will be a circle, while a tear-drop forms a rose bud; for others, such as tulips and bluebells, it is a bell. Roughly sketch this basic shape on to a piece of paper in pencil. Then build up details in colour within this boundary.

Practise painting on the paper first, using a good quality medium (size 4) brush and artists' acrylic colours. Aim for smooth, fluent strokes, starting at the fat end and tapering to a point.

Next time you have an opportunity, look closely at a real flower you want to paint, or a picture of one. Note the position of the shadows and the highlights; then with deep and paler paints you can pick out these shaded and lighter areas to give the bloom shape and form.

Stand back from your painting frequently to check the effect you are building up. Up close the results may seem very crude and un-flower-like; the long-distance impression is usually much more realistic.

Paint

Artist's acrylic paints are ideal. If you want the design to have a slightly faded appearance, you can mix colours by blending artist's acrylics with emulsion or artists' oils with eggshell – white for pastels, or a paler tone of the desired shade for deep, rich colours.

tip

Little pots of paint
Tiny tins of model painting enamel are an economical choice for small designs. They are available in a wide range of bright colours and dry to a hard-wearing finish.

▲ *Pretty as a picture* This modest cupboard deserves to take pride of place in any setting, thanks to the sunny, floral folk-art design featured on the drawer and door panel. Note on the drawer front how an orange knob is cleverly substituted for the main flower pattern that appears on the door.

a fine brush
for thin lines

a medium brush
for comma sweeps

a thick brush
for splotches

PAINTING FLOWERS

Daisy For a simple daisy shape, draw a free-hand circle 2.5-3.75cm (1-1½in) in diameter. Within the confines of this disc, paint in short, fat bluey-white petals radiating from a small, circular orange centre.

Thistle Paint a small circle in green. With a finer brush dipped in darker green paint, mark in small zigzags to represent the scales of the flower base. From the top of this circle stroke in fine purple lines rising from the crown as the petals of the thistle head.

Rose Draw a free-hand circle. Using a deep pink paint, twist two intertwined comma shapes for the closed, central petals. Swirl the remaining petals around this core. Grading to a slightly paler colour as you work out to the open petals adds form and realism.

Buttercup Sketch a small free-hand circle. Paint 4 or 5 bright yellow, slightly heart-shaped petals within this border. Finish off with a small bead of lime green in the centre.

Poppy Draw a free-hand circle. With a scarlet paint, divide this into four overlapping, cupped petals. Add a black spot for the centre.

Daffodil and narcissus Draw a circle with a conical or square bell in the middle to represent the trumpet sitting on its ruff of petals.

Bluebell and tulip For a head of bluebells, draw a number of small bells around a bent-over stem. Gradually make the bells slightly smaller as you work towards the tip. A tulip is an upside-down bell on the end of a straight stem.

Leaves Taking a medium brush, outline green pointed lozenges or droplets for leaves. Use a fine brush to add details like veins and stems.

▶ *Rest on your roses*
Inspired by the tablecloth and painted in blocks of strong colour, the bold images of roses transform a workaday chair into a pretty seat.

Materials
Artist's acrylic paints
Artist's brushes, fine, medium and thick
Clear polyurethane varnish
Paint brush

PAINTING A FLORAL MOTIF

1 Preparing the surface If the existing paintwork is in good condition, rub it over with fine glasspaper before painting. Taking all necessary precautions, strip any unsound paintwork back to the bare wood and sand it smooth before building up a new, strong finish with primer, undercoat and a matt topcoat. Tickle natural polished or varnished wooden surfaces with a very fine wire wool to key the surface for painting.

2 Arranging the design Position your colour plan on the piece to be decorated, using masking tape to hold it in place. Stand back to check the effect. When you are satisfied, trace the prominent features of the pattern on to the surface using dressmaker's carbon paper.

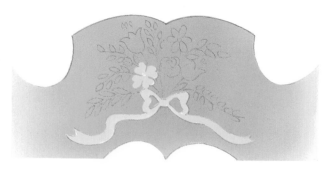

3 Starting to paint First paint the predominant part of the motif, in this case the yellow bow. Then fill in any other significant sections of the design to be painted in the same colour like the 'buttercup'. Save details such as the stamens of the tulip until the full shape has been painted in.

4 Building up the design Let the paint dry before moving on to the next part of the design. Clean the brush with each change of colour. Select the next notable part of the pattern, the rose in pink. Filling in this area now will help you to paint the rest of the flowers in their correct positions.

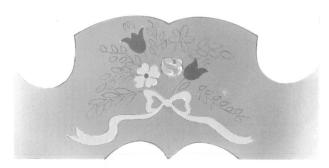

5 Flower arranging Using red paint, fill in the tulips on either side of the rose, again leaving the buds in red until later.

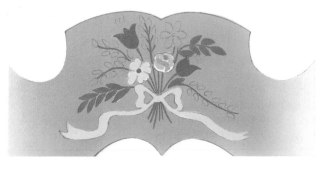

6 Adding stems and foliage The bouquet will really start to take shape when you add the green stems and leaves with a fine brush.

7 Putting on the detail Fill in the white petals of the daisy and the buds with quick swoops and dabs of the brush. Finally add the missing details in other colours.

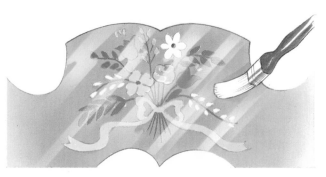

8 Protecting the surface Once complete and totally dry, finish off the decoration with 2 or 3 coats of clear polyurethane varnish.

Paint distressing

It is not altogether surprising that in an age when most new furniture is mass-produced, unique furniture designs and finishes are held in special regard. With our present-day interest in recreating an authentic period look in our homes, decorative painters have devised realistic ways of faking or simulating age on furniture. These techniques, known as distressing or antiquing, are easy to master, since you need no special equipment apart from paint brushes and glasspaper.

Methods of distressing

The word 'distressed' is used to describe the battered, slightly grazed appearance of the furniture rather than any specific techniques used to achieve this look. There is a variety of both techniques and paints that can be used, depending on the time and the type of paint available to you. You can work with oil-based paints which are resilient and easy to manipulate; eggshell is best because the shine of gloss paint is not really suitable for this technique. Alternatively, you may prefer to use water-based paints for their quick-drying properties; you don't have to worry about the dampness raising the grain of the wood since you will be sanding down the finish later.

But almost more important than the actual paint is your approach to its application. Remember you are aiming for a natural look. Understatement generally works better than overstating the effect; the more sensitive the handling and colour of the paint, the more convincing the aged quality of the piece of furniture will be, so be subtle with your distressing.

▲ **The art of ageing gracefully**
This sturdy sideboard looks as though it has been loved and enjoyed through generations of family life. Yet the same well-worn impression can be created in hours by deliberately distressing the paintwork by hand.

Choosing the items to be distressed

Distressing is a splendid technique for reviving plain, dull furniture. The best items to use are old pieces which have deteriorated too far to be restored to their original condition – simple cottage-style furniture or new pine furniture in traditional designs. Pieces of discarded junk, such as tables and chairs, emerge from distressing with renewed charm. Modern designs are not suitable because the style conflicts with the impression of ageing that you want.

Preparing the furniture

All the regular, common sense rules of preparing the surface for painting apply. Untreated wood needs the usual priming and undercoating before applying several coats of a thinned-down topcoat. Items which are already painted or varnished only need to be washed thoroughly and sanded down, in order to key the surface for further coats of paint. As you are aiming to simulate layers of paint acquired over the years, there is no point in stripping off existing ones just to replace them.

If a piece is cracked or knocked about in some way, so much the better, since it reinforces the impression of being time-worn. Some decorative painters even go so far as to damage the surface of the wood deliberately by knocking it with bunches of keys or a bag of stones in order to reproduce the wear and tear acquired from several generations of abuse. It is equally important that any furniture should be made safe.

Evidence of woodworm is an extra bonus, provided it has been treated and eradicated first. Woodworm holes can be faked using the finest bit from an electric drill. However, this should only be done after the final coat has been painted, otherwise the paint will fill the holes.

You may not feel that you want to resort to these drastic methods, but bear in mind that a new piece of untreated pine furniture with its crisp, clean edges will be harder to age than an old one with dents and scratches already.

◄ **Not so green** *Sanding a vivid green topcoat to uncover patches of lime and bare wood endows this plain chair with some endearing, elderly features.*

APPLYING AND SANDING OFF THE PAINT

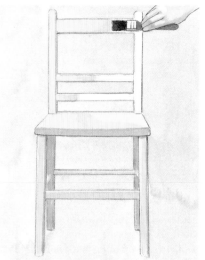

1 Preparing the surface Wash the chair thoroughly with warm, soapy water to remove dust and dirt. Scrape and sand away any blistered or flaking paint or varnish to create a sound surface. Wipe down with a clean cloth and allow to dry before painting. To give new wood a slightly damaged appearance, beat it with a bunch of keys or a bag of loose stones or coins.

2 Applying the basecoat Paint the chair all over in the base colour. If you are working on bare wood, you will need to apply a coat of primer first. Given the casual nature of the finished distressed effect, you don't have to put the basecoat on too thickly or evenly.

3 Putting on the topcoat Dilute the paint for the topcoat about three times with an appropriate thinner – water for emulsion and white spirit for eggshell. The topcoat should be fairly runny since, when dry, it will be rubbed down to allow the colour of the basecoat to show through in patches. When the basecoat is thoroughly dry, apply 2 or 3 layers of the topcoat, letting each one dry completely before putting on the next coat.

Selecting the colours

Once the piece of furniture has been satisfactorily prepared, the colours must then be carefully considered. 'Colours', as opposed to colour, is the operative word, since two colours are generally used. The whole idea of distressing is to allow the bottom layer of paint to grin through and be exposed in areas where an item would naturally receive the most wear.

Remember that the colour of a distressed piece of furniture is as important as the technique itself. The two colours to be used for paint distressing must complement each other; it doesn't matter whether you lay down the darker or lighter shade as the basecoat. Subtle colours, which are close to each other in tone, will work well, especially the duller, more earthy ones. But strong colours work equally well, particularly in à for furniture in a sunny setting.

Many modern paints tend to be rather brash for an antiqued finish. To look believably old, colours should be dirtied or muddied. As a rough guide, bright blues should have

a touch of orange added to them; pinks and reds should have green mixed in and yellows should have a tinge of purple added, and vice versa. In other words, any colour will be toned down by its complementary partner.

Alternatively, the addition of the pigment raw umber in the form of universal stainer is a good substitute, since it will tone down any colour and can be mixed with both oil and water-based paints. It can also be used in a glaze or thin wash over a topcoat to imitate the accumulation of years of patina.

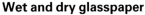

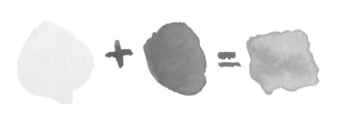

4 Sanding down the surface Your aim now is to create a worn topcoat. After the final coat of paint has dried, take a piece of fine glasspaper and rub the paint surface. Sand down to the basecoat in some places and through to the bare wood in others, while retaining areas of top coat intact. From time to time, it is a good idea to wipe the piece down, stand back and look at the overall effect you are producing.

5 Distressing the finish While you are rubbing down the surface, think about where the piece in front of you would suffer wear under normal circumstances. In general, give exposed areas along the edges and mouldings and around handles or knobs extra attention with slightly deeper rubbing so that the surface looks unevenly worn. On the chair, concentrate on the top back rail, where it might have been handled most, and around the base of the legs, which could have been knocked frequently by shoes or a broom.

6 Waxing the surface When you are satisfied with the result, either wash or wipe the piece down thoroughly. Then rub furniture wax all over the surface with a clean, dry cloth. Buff to a sheen with another soft cotton cloth. Repeat the waxing process for extra protection and lustre. Alternatively, use a satin or matt varnish to protect the surface. Avoid a high gloss finish as this is far too shiny and new-looking for this paint effect.

◄ An illusion of age
A kitchen cabinet and table seem to bear the scrapes of long, hard service. In this case, however, looks are deceptive: ageing is under the control of the decorator who has sanded the red paint down to a pale undercoat and lashed the surface of the table into a convincing but premature old age.

▼ Frayed edging
The weather-beaten quality of distressed paintwork works well on small items too. The slightly faded effect on these picture frames is ideally suited to displaying a collection of seashore souvenirs.

▼ Deeply distressed The finished result of distressing a piece of furniture depends on how far you want to take the sanding-off technique. At its most drastic, on this wall cupboard for instance, bare wood vies for as much attention as the painted surface and the arrangement of the worn areas becomes a major design consideration.

Liming wood

Although it's now a very fashionable paint effect liming is in fact an old, traditional finish which was used in redecorating farmhouses every year during the annual spring-cleaning. It was a rough finish, carried out by farmers and peasants who couldn't afford the luxury of more elaborate decorations. Initially the walls were treated with the liming solution and any remaining mixture was then diluted for use on the woodwork. Since lime is extremely caustic in its wet state, liming cleansed the houses of bugs and bacteria – the equivalent of today's disinfectant. By the time spring came round again, the lime would have worn away, ready for a fresh application.

Although white limewash was most commonly used, occasionally a pigment might be added to the lime to give it a colour. These colours were often regionally traditional, so that in one area the limewash was sometimes a light green, whereas in another a yellow ochre was added. In fact, all over Europe, as far apart as Greece, Denmark and Czechoslovakia, as well as in America, pigments were added to a basic white limewash to give a characteristic local colour to the walls.

▼ In soft focus
The oak furniture in this bedroom has been limed, mimicking the typically light, misty quality of faded wood, to match the white sheer drape at the window, the pale, colour-washed walls and the pastel-stained floorboards.

paint

soft cloth

wire wool

rubber gloves

wire brush

paint brush

furniture wax

The effect of liming

In England, the furniture in humble houses and cottages was often made from oak. Both oak and pitch pine were the most usual woods to be limed. They were widely used and had a coarse grain which took the lime well. Limed oak and pine were treated with a mixture containing lime putty. Authentic liming is rather a hazardous technique to carry out, since lime is so caustic, but there are various other modern techniques which imitate the effect. They are just as attractive and all the more satisfactory for using safer materials.

Liming gives a whitened or bleached look to the wood while allowing the grain to show through, as though it has faded naturally from standing out in the sun and rain. The liming shows up best on wide, prominently grained woods and can be used in your home on floors and doors as well as furniture. The soft, subtle effect works particularly well in neutral colour schemes in town or country interiors because it adds interesting texture to the designs.

Suitable furniture

Oak is a naturally pale-coloured wood which can look very dull and sombre, especially on 1930s furniture where it is often covered in a dark treacle-like varnish. In this state it can look extremely ugly and sober, so you need a sensitive eye to recognize the potential of these pieces. Go for simple classic lines and shapes. You can often find oak and other highly grained wood furniture at reasonable prices in junk shops.

All varnish or paint should be thoroughly removed prior to liming; this is best done using a proprietary stripper. Alternatively, various workshops will do the stripping by a dipping method for you. Ring round and get several quotes first because prices can vary greatly.

Stripping with a blow torch is not recommended since any scorch marks will show up against the pale wood. Look out for environmentally friendly strippers that are less noxious to use and won't harm your skin.

Methods of liming

You can buy liming kits and mix up a traditional liming solution or you can use white eggshell paint or liming wax to simulate the ancient liming technique without any of the original caustic complications. Both the wax and paint are easy and cheap to apply, with liming wax producing a more subtle limed-wood effect with a softer sheen than the white paint.

Wear rubber gloves to protect your hands and remember to wear old clothes or a protective apron. If you are liming indoors, take the precaution of spreading newspaper or a dust sheet around to safeguard the floor. Painting can be messy and you should avoid dropping any liming wax on the floor.

▼ Light-heartedly
Giving this little dressing table a limed finish imparts it with a charming delicacy that looks most appropriate in a bedroom.

Materials
Paint or **varnish stripper, a paint brush, scraper** and a sheet of **fine glasspaper**
Stiff **wire brush**
White eggshell paint plus optional colouring agents such as **universal stainers** or **oil-based pigments**
Rubber gloves
Cotton cloth and **white spirit**
Furniture wax and **soft cloth**
For liming with wax:
Fine **steel wool,** 000 grade
Tin of **liming wax**

LIMING WITH PAINT

1 Cleaning the piece Remove any varnish or paint from the wood which is to be limed with a proprietary stripper, following all the recommended precautions. If necessary take a sheet of fine glasspaper to sand away any traces of dark varnish in the wood.

2 Raising the grain Take a strong, decorator's wire brush and brush it firmly in the direction of the grain to accentuate it and remove any soft wood. Wipe away any resulting dust.

3 Applying the paint Wearing rubber gloves, dip a cloth into the eggshell paint, previously tinted to a pale colour if you wish. Rub the paint over the wood, making certain to work the paint well into the grain.

4 Wiping off the paint Take a clean cloth slightly dampened in white spirit and, working along the surface, wipe off the excess paint so that colour is left only in the grain. Allow to dry thoroughly.

5 Finishing the surface The surface can be left as it is, or furniture wax can be rubbed all over with a soft cloth and then buffed off again to give a resilient surface with a slight sheen.

tip

Colourful liming
If you want to add a subtle hint of colour to your liming effect, choose a coloured eggshell paint. Alternatively, mix your own shade, using universal stainers or artist's oil colours to tint the eggshell.

Pour a little paint from the tin into a jam jar and experiment with the mixing first. Even a small amount of colour will have an obvious effect so be careful not to add too much. Pale blue-greys and greeny greys are the most traditional shades.

Applying a limed effect over wood that has already been stained in a vivid colour produces an impressive effect which you can co-ordinate with your existing design scheme.

LIMING WITH WAX

1 Preparing the surface Before liming, remove all the varnish or paint from the wood with a proprietary stripper, taking all recommended precautions. Raise the grain with a stiff wire brush, as before. Then wipe away any dust.

2 Applying the liming wax Wearing rubber gloves, pull a piece of fine steel wool from the roll, form it into a small pad and dip it into the liming wax. Rub the liming wax into the wood, applying it with and against the grain to make sure that all the indentations in the wood grain are filled.

3 Completing the waxing After a while the steel wool will become soaked with wax and you will need to use a fresh pad and dip that in liming wax before continuing. Cover the whole article, making sure that the wax is well pushed into every corner until it looks white all over. Leave the item to soak for 30 minutes. The longer it is left, the more pronounced and grainy the eventual effect will be.

4 Waxing the liming wax Next, take another fresh piece of steel wool and dip it into a tin of wax furniture polish. Rub this over the surface in order to remove the liming wax. When you have been over the whole piece, buff the wax up with a soft cotton cloth. This gives a soft, lustrous sheen to the finish which can be re-waxed and polished at intervals to give continuous protection.

Liming around the home

The cool, faded appearance of liming can be used to great effect around the house not only for restoring old furniture but also for mellowing new. It will add a softness to bare boards and exposed beams and cast an enchanting dusky glow over smaller wooden objects like picture and mirror frames, lamp bases, bowls and boxes.

▶ In the limelight
With its liming treatment applied over a grey stain, a heavy, old wooden desk fits in perfectly with the muted shades of this library-like decor. Liming has filled the open grain with white colouring to create an intriguing, grey-veined pattern over the surface.

◀ Thistle-down
Liming gives the oak frame of this handsome, rush-seated chair a weathered elegance which would be well suited to a colour scheme using other natural materials, like bleached floorboards or coir matting, and colour-washed walls.

▼ Cooking with lime The clean, bleached appearance of limed wood is an extremely popular finish for traditional-looking kitchen units. Here, the liming technique has been used to display the patterns in the grain of the wood more clearly and highlight the mouldings on the door panels, drawer fronts and turned corner spindles.

Painting wooden floors

Of all flooring alternatives, plain wooden boards offer the greatest scope for inventiveness and fun. After sanding, you can apply numerous decorative finishes – wax, varnish, stain or paint – to the spotless bare boards to make them more hard-wearing and look more interesting. One exciting option is to paint a bold geometric pattern all over the floor. This is most simply achieved by blanking off a grid design on the floor with masking tape. You can either lay the pattern over the natural wood or paint the bare boards in a background colour before applying the design. Even when worked simply, in just a couple of colours, the results can look extremely effective and original.

▲ Ring of posies
An enterprising use of painted images and a marbled paint effect in startling greens produces a striking overall impression in this kitchen. In particular, the floral garland painted on the woodstrip floor makes a strong focal feature of the table and chairs by containing the area within a rug-like circle.

Planning the design

Before you start painting, it is crucial to plan and map out the design grid accurately. Measure the dimensions of the room and draw yourself a scaled-down outline on a piece of paper. To make life simpler if the room is an irregular shape, you can work out the largest rectangle that will fit into the space and arrange the pattern within it.

Most patterns – squares, criss-cross, herring-bone, triangular, diamond, hexagonal and star – are based on a grid of lines drawn at 30°, 45°, 60° or 90° to the boards. Practise on a piece of paper to assess the results of using different angles, spacings and colours. Use a school protractor or set square to fix the angles. To ensure that the pattern lines coincide with the floorboards, let the width of a floorboard determine the scale of the design. Depending on the size of pattern you want and the width of each floorboard, set the lines either two, three or four board-widths apart.

Decide on the design and choose the colour scheme. Bear in mind that large patterns and dark colours will make a room seem smaller, while more detailed patterns and light colours amplify the feeling of space. Map the outline of the pattern on to your room plan to make sure that the main features of the design fall in sensible places, centring the pattern on the wall against which it will be most conspicuous.

Types of finish

A floor probably suffers from more wear and tear than any other surface in the house. So any finish has to be hardwearing and resistant to scuffing. You can use normal home-decorating gloss or eggshell paints, with their appropriate primers and undercoats to build up a durable finish. Special floor paints give a more resilient finish but are only available in a limited range of colours. Marine paints are exceptionally durable but take a long time to dry. The pattern can also be carried out in wood stain or coloured varnish. In all cases, it is a good idea to add a final coat or two of clear varnish to the surface once it is dry for extra protection.

Using masking tape

Masking tape is ideal for creating geometric designs. Apply in straight lines for a simple striped border, or cut up short lengths to lay down as zigzags,

triangles, diamonds or squares. Low-tack masking tape is designed to be easily detachable after use, without taking any paint off with it. Alternatively, remove some of the stickiness from ordinary masking tape by patting it up and down on a piece of cotton fabric before applying it. You can buy masking tape from art and decorating supply stores in a number of different widths.

Materials

Pencil and **paper**, **protractor** or **set square** and **string**
5cm (2in) broad **low-tack masking tape**
Paint brushes
Gloss, **eggshell**, **floor** or **marine paint** in the colours of the pattern
Clear one-coat, quick-drying **varnish**
Craft knife and **metal rule** for scoring the floor when using wood stains

PAINTING A FLOOR

This is a simple pattern of pale blue squares and cream lines criss-crossed over the floor. More complicated designs can be masked out in exactly the same way using different angles.

1 Preparing the boards Clear the room completely and sand down the boards to a clean, smooth finish, removing all traces of dust.

2 Painting the boards If you want to paint the design straight on to plain wooden boards, proceed to Step 3. For an all-over background colour, apply a coat of primer to the boards before brushing on a coat of undercoat followed by at least two coats of topcoat in the design colour – in this case cream. Leave to dry.

► Simple ground rules
Even a basic lattice pattern painted underfoot can make a dramatic impact when executed in a couple of fresh colours over the whole floor.

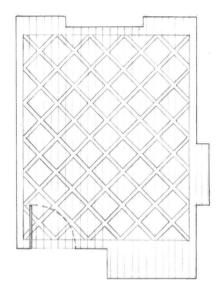

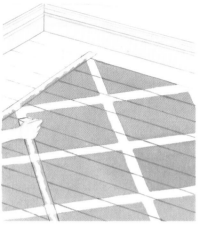

8 Pulling off the masking tape Let the paint dry thoroughly before lifting the masking tape and touching up any imperfections for a clean edge to the pattern.

3 Mapping out the design Draw an outline of your pattern on a diagram of the room before you start marking out the floor. Following your plan closely, first lay down the perimeter of the pattern in masking tape, if appropriate. Then mark out the intervals of the design.

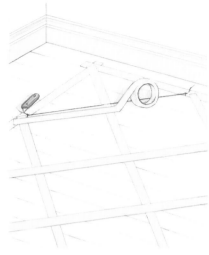

6 Completing the pattern Repeat the whole scheme from the left-hand corner, working at 45° in the opposite direction across the boards to create a criss-cross pattern.

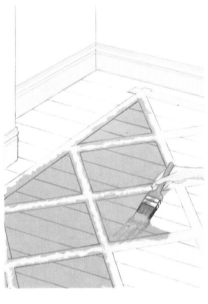

9 Protecting the paint Brush a protective coat of clear varnish over the whole floor surface.

4 Laying the first line Starting in the far right-hand corner of the room, pin a piece of string to the floor, against the skirting or on the edge of the patterned area, 2.5cm (1in) to the right of the corner, so the tape is centred on the corner when it is laid. Using a set square as a guide, stretch the string across the room at 45° to the opposite wall. Using this string as a guideline, lay down a 5cm (2in) wide strip of masking tape across the floor.

5 Building up the design Now move the string to the right along the wall or edge by 3 or 4 board-widths and repeat the procedure until you have a series of parallel taped lines running at 45° across one half of the room. Then go back to the beginning and tape a set of lines to the left of the original line over the other half of the floor.

7 Painting the grid Starting in the corner furthest from the door, apply the blue paint to the un-masked squares. You can daub over the tape; it won't show later.

10 Caring for the floor Keep a painted or varnished floor clean with regular vacuuming. Use a damp cloth to remove marks. For additional protection, you can apply an emulsion-based polish every two or three months, either by hand or with an electric polisher.

 tip

Scoring the pattern
When using coloured dyes to create the pattern on the boards, prevent the stain from running across the margins of the outline by scoring carefully along the edges of masking tape with a sharp craft knife. Use a metal rule to guide the blade in a straight line and prevent it slipping or jumping dangerously as you lightly mark the floor.

Alternative floor treatments

Stencils For a more ambitious design, you can use a stencil for transferring a colourful pattern to the floor, perhaps linking it to stencilling on the walls or furniture.

Borders When a rug fills the centre of a room, you may only want to paint or varnish a pattern around a border.

'Rugs' Conversely, you may only wish to paint the design as a mock rug under a table or in front of a fire.

Liming For a mellow, bleached effect, you could apply a limed finish to the bare boards by rubbing in liming wax and leaving it to dry before buffing off with wax polish. Another method is to apply a coat of white paint over the surface and then to use a clean cloth to wipe off all but a thin film of paint in the grain. Work over a small area at a time so that the paint does not dry before you wipe it off. Seal the finish with wax polish or a coat of clear matt varnish (see pages 33–36).

▼ On a grand scale
The chequer, tile-like pattern on the wooden boards in this hallway shows that painted floors are just as at home in grand locations as in more humble abodes. Regardless of scale, the method of masking the design remains the same.

► Ley lines
A painted floor pattern can play a valuable co-ordinating role in linking designs and colours from room to room, or within one room. Here, the blue of the bedroom rug has been repeated in a border round the adjacent room.

Crackle glazing

One sure suggestion of mellow antiquity is the lovely, complex web of fine cracks that appears over the surface of old furniture and oil paintings and on the ageing paintwork of walls and doors. Crackle glazing simulates this subtly crazed effect artificially by applying incompatible layers of paint or varnish to the surface. By mimicking the results of timeworn maturity so accurately, you can also lessen the stark contrast between newly painted or restored items and truly old ones that have cracked and faded naturally.

The genuinely crackled surface on painted furniture or oil paintings has been formed over the years by the layers of different finishes drying out at varying rates or being exposed to changes in temperature and humidity. In oil paintings, for example, the paint takes much longer than the protective coat of varnish to dry. Therefore, when the paint slowly shrinks as it dries it causes the hardened, brittle varnish on top to crack. Dust then lodges in the cracks emphasizing them and increasing the aged appearance.

▼ Going crazy
The intricate patterns of hairline cracks tracing across the surface of these painted pebbles, shells and wooden bowl clearly illustrate the crazed effects of crackle glazing.

Methods of crackle glazing

Crackle-glaze techniques were first developed in France in the 18th century to replicate and speed up the effects of the gradual process of drying out. With the varnish method, a quick-drying, water-based varnish is applied over a slower-drying oil varnish, causing the surface to crack. The cracks produced by the interactions of the two different types of varnish are so fine that they are almost invisible until a tinted oil glaze is deliberately rubbed in to pick them out. Crackle varnish is particularly suitable for use on an already painted or papered surface, which will be visible beneath the varnish. This makes it an ideal finish for a découpaged screen or box.

The crackle paint effect works in a similar way, with the top coat of paint cracking and shrinking back to reveal a layer of different coloured paint beneath. Use subdued colours to create an impression of age. Alternatively, employ bold colours for a purely decorative, fun effect.

Crackle paint effect

Any item which can be painted is suitable for crackle paint treatment – door or cupboard frames, lamp bases, gift boxes or picture frames. Do not use this paint effect on containers that are used for food, as water-based paints will not stand up to regular washing. It is always worth experimenting with colours and technique before you start in earnest. This finish shows up most effectively when contrasting colours are applied or when it is used more discreetly to display different tones of the same colour. Remember that chinks of background colour may be lost if there is too subtle a shade difference.

The technique

For a crackle paint effect, a base coat of ordinary household emulsion paint is painted over the surface and allowed to dry. This is then covered with a layer of transparent gum arabic. When dry, a second colour emulsion is brushed over it. Speedy application is essential as the water in the emulsion paint soon softens the dry gum arabic. In order to get the desired crazed effect, the layers must not mix. Amazingly, the top layer starts to crack within seconds to reveal the base colour through the slits.

The gum arabic is the magic ingredient that compels the top coat to shrink and split open. Complete crackle paint kits are available from large art and craft shops. Most art supply shops sell water-colour gum arabic. You can also buy crystals which need to be dissolved in boiling water and then left to stand overnight to thicken slightly before they are used.

Since any crackle glazing method ends with a water-based layer, the surface needs some further protection to make it more resilient. You can either use matt or satin polyurethane varnish or buff it to a luminous sheen with beeswax polish on a soft cloth.

▼ **Colour effects**
Results range from the subtle to the dramatic.

▲ **Deceptively old**
The network of splits produced by crackle painting looks so convincing that it can be difficult to tell whether a surface is truly old – like the background panelling – or deliberately aged – as on the frame.

Materials

Emulsion paint in two colours
12mm (½in) **paint brushes**
Water-colour gum arabic
Washing-up liquid

CRACKLE PAINTING

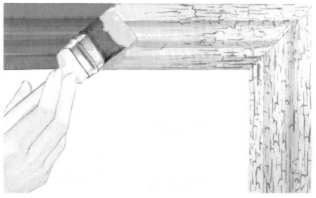

1 **Putting on the base colour** Prepare the surface of the item to be painted so that it is clean, dry and completely free from grease. On bare wood or metal, apply a coat of primer. Then brush on a coat of the first colour emulsion and leave to dry thoroughly.

2 **Applying the gum arabic** Add a small drop of washing-up liquid to the gum arabic to stop it separating when applied to the surface and mix well. Brush gum arabic over the entire surface. Leave to dry.

3 **Painting the top coat** Quickly and evenly paint a second colour emulsion over the surface. Do not go over the same area more than once as this will spoil the previous layers. Cracks start to appear almost instantly – you can use a hair-dryer to speed up the process and make bigger cracks in the top layer of paint.

4 **Protecting the finish** For a finer crackled finish, repeat steps 2 and 3. Finally, apply a couple of coats of varnish or rub wax into the surface to protect it from wear and tear. A gloss finish makes bright colours shine while subtle shades glow under a soft sheen.

tip

Crazier patterns
The manner in which you brush on the gum arabic or crackle varnish influences the nature of the crackling; brushing in a haphazard fashion creates the craziest, most chaotic crackle.

▼ *Get cracking Small objects, like these wooden balls, are ideal for practising the crackle painting technique and experimenting with different colour combinations.*

Crackle varnish effect

Crackle varnish is available in a two-part pack, which contains two different varnishes. The slow-drying oil-based varnish is applied first. The quicker drying water-based varnish is then brushed over the top. You can create your own crackle varnish combination by using an ordinary oil-based varnish with a water-based one. Experiment first, in case you do not attain the required effect immediately.

After varnishing, artist's oil paint is rubbed into the surface to point up the cracks. To mimic accumulated dirt, use dark, earthy colours like raw umber or burnt sienna. Thin the oil paint with a little white spirit and rub it lightly over the surface with a brush. Excess paint can then be removed with a cloth, leaving a dark film in the cracks.

▶ *Instant ageing The tray has certainly gained extra character as a result of the mellowing effect of the crackle varnish and muddy glaze applied to its surface.*

Materials

Crackle varnish pack or two incompatible types of varnish; one oil-based and one water-based
Two 12-25mm (½-1in) **paint brushes**
Artist's oil paint for picking out the cracks
White spirit and **cotton rags**

CRACKLE VARNISHING

1 Applying the first varnish Brush a thin coat of the oil-based varnish all over the finished surface in a very even layer. If necessary, dilute the varnish slightly with a little white spirit. Allow to dry until the surface is just tacky to the touch; this usually takes 1-2 hours, depending on temperature and humidity.

2 Putting on the second varnish Quickly cover the entire coat of the first varnish with a thick layer of the second, water-based varnish and leave to dry. The cracking becomes more obvious if you use a hair-dryer.

3 Correcting the effect When the varnish is dry, and if you are satisfied with the finish created by the two varnishes, proceed to Step 4. If as the varnish dries, the cracking is very fine and subtle, the layer on the first varnish was too dry when the second varnish was applied. In this case, wipe off the second varnish quickly with a damp cloth and repeat Steps 1 and 2, leaving less time between applying the two coats.

4 Coating with artist's oil paint Mix the chosen artist's oil colour paint with a little of the first oil-based varnish. Using a rag, rub this gently over the whole surface and work it well into all the cracks.

5 Removing excess oil paint With a clean, dry cloth, carefully remove the excess oil colour from the surface, leaving a thin residue in the cracks.

6 Protecting the surface Allow the final finish to dry for 3-7 days. Then protect with two coats of oil-based varnish or rub wax in thoroughly all over the surface.

Marbling

Marble, with its cool, translucent sheen and delicately veined surface, is a very special material – costly to buy, difficult to handle and a challenge to work with. Naturally enough, these particular qualities have placed marble into the realms of extravagance and grandeur, so as might be expected, there has always been an interest in simulating the effect with less expensive materials like paints and glazes.

Looking at marble

The characteristic vein formations in marble are caused by the tremendous pressures which occur during its slow transformation from basic limestone. The variations of colour and stratified patterns are enormous – from cool greys and creams through to greens and rich-red earthy shades. To capture the subtle qualities of marble its soft cloudiness, colour, pattern and texture – look at real examples of the material, or at least at pictures, to familiarize yourself with these features and with traditional applications.

Because of its weight, marble used on a grand scale for interior decoration has traditionally been pieced together in slabs and slim panels. Colour-matched sections are used this way to present a

▲ Grand illusions
Marble paint effects bestow an aura of elegance – perfect for creating a formal style in entrance halls or sitting rooms. Rich warm colours balance the grand effect beautifully.

uniform effect, giving the appearance of a solid expanse on walls and floors. Large areas of one colour are often integrated in a design and surrounded by border patterns or friezes created with shapes cut from marble in contrasting colours. For realistic marble effects, copy these applications when planning your own designs.

▲ **Dramatic dados**
Fake and fantasy are combined here to create a realistic marble effect on wall panelling. Note how the wall and marble colours complement each other.

Creating marble effects

Faux, or false, marbling can be used to imitate 'the real thing', on fireplaces, walls and floors, or to create a theatrical, almost surreal surface on doors and furniture.

To achieve these results, layers of paint in subtly graded colours are applied with a sponge, rag or brush to represent the base colour of the marble. The distinctive dark veins are traced on top and painted in with a fine brush. They are then blurred and softened with a dry brush or feather, or by sponging.

Before starting work on a project, build up confidence on a small practice piece, or with a sample board. Mistakes will probably not be noticed, but those that are can usually be removed by wiping the paint away, or by blending the error into the design with a dry brush. Aim to work quickly and lightly, in a relaxed way, so that the effect takes on a spontaneous, lively quality.

A bath panel, fireplace surround or picture frame are ideal surfaces to try out the marble effect before embarking on larger scale projects. When planning to cover large areas like walls or floors, take a tip from the way marble is traditionally used and divide the area up into blocks and panels with a pencil and ruler. Each panel can then be painted individually which is easier than trying to paint over a wide expanse. The results will give a subtle change in colour and pattern over the whole area.

Using oil or water paints

Convincing marble effects can be worked with oil or water-based paints. The same basic tools and equipment are used for each method and both paint finishes require a protective top coat of varnish to create a surface sheen.

The main advantage of using water-based paints like emulsion or artist's acrylic paint or gouache is speed but the paints are also considered easier to use. To make the process even simpler, marbling kits with water-based paints are available in pre-selected colour combinations. These offer a choice of natural marble shades or exciting fantasy

---

A MARBLE EFFECT

1 Applying the base coat Paint the background surface with a coat of white paint. Leave to dry, then very carefully rub it over with glasspaper or wire wool. This roughens the surface slightly to provide a 'key'.

2 Tinting the base coat In a glass jar mix a glaze of two parts white paint and one part white spirit (or water). Tint with a small squeeze of raw umber and a little black. Mix to create a pale grey shade. (If the result is too dark, simply add a little more white and thin as necessary with white spirit or water.) Paint over the prepared surface with a 50mm (2in) paint brush.

3 Dappling the colour While the paint is still wet, use a sponge or a piece of rolled rag to dab away some of the colour to reveal at least 50 per cent of the base coat.

4 Adding more tint While the previous coat is still damp, mix some more base colour and tint. Use a little more black and less umber this time or introduce another colour like raw sienna or yellow ochre. This helps to achieve a subtle contrast. Dab on the colour at random with a sponge or rag to add depth to the effect. Leave to dry.

5 Marking on marble veins Draw a veining design on to tracing paper. Take the design from a piece of real marble if possible. Trail the main veins diagonally right across the tracing, then branch smaller veins out from these and link them to other veins. Place the tracing over the base surface and anchor it with tape. Slip the carbon paper underneath and trace off the veins. To transfer the design over large areas, stagger the position of the tracing so that the design does not repeat itself in a straight line. Join in the vein ends unobtrusively.

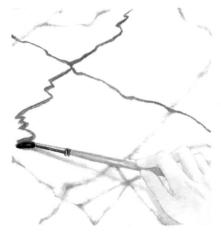

6 Painting the veins Mix raw umber and a little black together to produce a brownish-grey tint. Hold a fine paint-brush loosely and, with a light, almost shaky touch, paint along some of the marked lines. While still wet, remove excess paint by dabbing over the veins with a dampened sponge or rag (use white spirit or water, as appropriate). While the first veins are still wet, mix a dark grey tint and paint more veins as before, following the veining map.

carbon paper

veining pattern

French chalk

artist's paints

Artist's oil colours in raw umber, black, raw sienna and yellow ochre (or emulsion paint, artist's acrylic or gouâche in the same colours)

White spirit to thin oil paints to a glaze (or water for water-based paints)

Sea sponge and **lint-free cotton rags**

Household paint brushes Use a **large brush** for the background colour and a 50mm (2in) **decorator's brush** and one or two **artist's watercolour brushes** with fine points for the details

Fine glasspaper or **fine gauge wire wool** to prepare painted base surface for following paint details

Glass jar for thinning paint and an **old plate** for mixing colours

Varnish Choose a matt or satin-finish clear polyurethane varnish

French chalk to rub into completed paint effect to give a marble-like sheen

Tracing paper to make a veining map

Well-used carbon paper (so transferred image is soft), **low-tack tape, soft lead pencil** and **ruler** to transfer the veining map to the base surface

Rubber gloves to protect hands

colours. However, to achieve marble effects with the greatest density of colours and translucency, oil-based paints are the traditional choice. The instructions given on these pages describe how to create a naturalistic white marble effect with grey-brown veining. Vary the colour combinations to suit a particular decorating scheme.

Materials

Base surfaces Plaster, wallpaper, wood chipboard, plywood, medium density fibreboard and hardboard are all suitable. These should be prepared and primed using the appropriate materials.

Base colour paint Use oil-based eggshell (or water-based emulsion) paint in a soft white shade

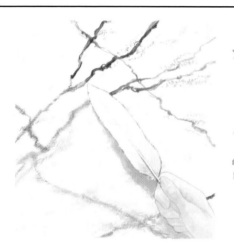

7 Adding more veins Work smaller veins using a mixture of these two tints, or mix different colours; each tint should contrast slightly with the ground colour. Then with a feather or dry brush, stroke gently back and forth across each line to soften the effect.

Improvise for effect
Try using dry or dampened foam-tipped make-up applicators and large blusher brushes to soften the edges of the marble veins. Small make-up sponges have a very fine texture and can be useful adding small, subtle variations in colour.

8 Softening the background Use a dry sponge or rag to absorb excess colour while the paint is still damp. Dab this excess on to the background 'marble', to give the impression of subtle variegations.

9 Softening the effect While the veins are still wet, gently work a dry paint brush or feather across the veins to soften the outline. Repeat until the veins have a delicately blurred outline, then work over the entire surface in the same way.

10 Painting small details When the surface is dry, thin some white paint and lightly work some very small veins and tiny sponged patches into the design. Leave to dry completely for at least 24 hours.

11 Adding a sheen Use a 50mm (2in) brush to apply an even coat of polyurethane varnish. When this is almost dry, sprinkle with French chalk. Rub this in with a soft lint-free cloth to give the painted surface a sheen like real marble.

Small scale marble effects

Accessories like lamp bases or trays and small pieces of furniture – tables, chests of drawers or chairs – are ideal subjects for first experiments with marble paint effects. They are excellent for creating a dramatic impact in a small or sparsely furnished space, as their quirky good looks are bound to invite favourable comment.

▶ **Draw up a chair**
These simple wooden chairs have been given an unexpected new image with coloured marble effect frames. The marble veins are painted on to the wood using especially designed water-based marble paint kits. The colour range makes it easy to create clever mix and match options, and to link different styles and sizes.

▼ **Fantasy fake**
Marble paint effects offer the opportunity to transform a junk shop 'find' like this chest of drawers into a conversation piece. When traditional renovations prove too costly, a detailed marble design, worked in colours to complement the decor, can give a new lease of life to a favourite piece of furniture.

Painting texture on to walls

The rustic simplicity of a rough plaster wall immediately brings to mind the ambience of country living. Very few people are fortunate enough to live with the genuine article but, with a little time, effort and imagination, it is now possible to achieve similar effects using modern texture finishes.

These texture coverings are extremely versatile and, with proper preparation, can be applied to almost any surface. For some finishes, the texture pattern is created as it goes on; with others, you sculpt the coating afterwards, using special tools to create all manner of effects. In addition to their decorative

▲ Roughly country
A crudely textured wall and painted brickwork combine to create a convincingly rustic setting.

appeal, texture finishes can be used to cover a multitude of cracks and defects on walls.

Texture finishes

Texture coverings offer a choice of wall finishes, depending on which type you use and how you apply it. Some have quite a gritty texture more suited to ceilings than walls, since they are abrasive to the touch and hard to clean. Others are smooth until you texture the surface.

You can mix powdered forms to almost any consistency, which enables you to obtain a variety of textures. When dry they can be painted to give a water-resistant, wipe-clean finish.

There is also a range of ready-mixed products available, which are almost as versatile as the powder form. Used straight from the tub, they can be applied by brush or roller and textured as desired. They dry to a matt white, washable finish, making them ideal for use where there is condensation.

Both types of texture finish possess elastic qualities that can resist cracking often associated with building movement.

Materials

Glasspaper and **sponge** or **cloth** for cleaning the surface
General purpose plaster filler, filler knife and **sealer**
Dust sheets or **plastic sheeting** for protecting the floor
Texture paint applied with a **large paint brush** or **foam** or **fibre roller** and a **small paint brush**
Texturing tools – sponge, stippling brush, comb or sculpted roller for creating textured patterns
Emulsion paint, paint brush and **cloth**

TEXTURING A WALL

1 Preparing the wall Good preparation of the wall surface is essential. Remove all flaking and dusty material, distemper, wallpaper and paste. Lightly sand any gloss surfaces. Then wash the surface with soapy water and leave to dry.

2 Filling in cracks If the surface is badly cracked, fill in with a good quality, general purpose plaster filler and leave to dry.

3 Sealing the wall Any absorbent surfaces, such as plasterboard, new plasterwork and surfaces freshly stripped of wallpaper and paint, should be sealed with an appropriate primer.

▼ **Rolling ripples** Reminiscent of the sea, this cool blue bathroom wall has been skilfully textured using a special sculpted rubber roller.

4 Experimenting with design Before you begin applying the texture covering to the wall or ceiling, always practise the texturing technique on a piece of hardboard until you get the effect you want.

▼ **Sunny stucco** This subtle, roughened pattern on the wall, created by applying the texture covering with a large, generously loaded paint brush, cleverly conveys the impression of a Mediterranean stucco finish.

50

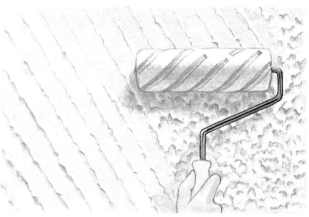

5 **Applying the covering to the wall** Using a large paint brush or roller, apply a generous coat of the covering to about 1 square metre (1 square yard) at a time, using slow, deliberate strokes.

6 **Texturing the surface** With your chosen texturing tool, texture this area of the surface. Then repeat steps 5 and 6 until the whole area is covered with a roughened pattern.

7 **Finishing the edges** When you have finished texturing the wall or ceiling, paint a narrow margin of texture finish round the edges with a 12-25mm (½-1in) paint brush. You can leave this as a plain border or introduce matching texture by hand. Leave to dry for 7 days.

8 **Distressing the wall** To create a soft effect, apply a pale coloured paint, such as cream or soft yellow, to the textured wall. Then, while the paint is still wet, roll a clean rag into a loose ball and lightly remove areas of the painted surface to produce mellow mottling.

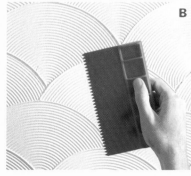

Alternative effects

You can create a variety of patterns with different tools.

Stippling (A) Use a texturing brush on the newly applied covering to create a stippled effect. Dab on and off the wall, bringing the tool away cleanly, to avoid drag marks.

Combing (B) A texturing comb can create a number of effects, including fans and concentric circles. Place the comb's teeth into freshly applied covering, then turn through semi-circles.

Brushing (C) Pulling a large paint brush through the finish is a way of applying a random roughness to any surface.

Sponging (D) A household sponge makes a good tool for texturing walls. Dab the finish with a coarse sponge to form a finely stippled effect. To create a swirling pattern, place the sponge into the freshly applied covering and rotate it firmly and steadily in a circle. Lift off cleanly and repeat.

Design options

When linked with a stone coloured paint, a textured finish presents opportunities to create realistic imitation stone effects. These can range from the regular, monumental blocks used to build castles and mansions to the rugged boulders that form the walls of rural cottages. Your strategy will depend on the look you want for your home.

CREATING STONE BLOCKS

1 Roughening up the surface After preparing the wall, brush on the texture covering and then finely stipple to create a roughened stone effect. Leave to dry.

2 Painting the walls Paint over the textured finish with a stone coloured paint. While the paint is wet, rub some of it off again with a cloth to give a weathered look.

▼ *Mock block*
Here, the striking 'stone' walls are achieved by applying a blotchy paint effect on a lightly stippled surface.

3 Creating stone blocks To mock up the appearance of stone blocks – a technique known as *faux ashlar* – carefully draw out a grid on the wall to establish the size and position of the blocks. Paint over this outline with an off-white paint so you can see the block arrangement.

4 Completing the effect To give the blocks a subtle, three-dimensional appearance, shade around two edges of each block with a slightly darker paint, which effectively throws them into relief.

Removing texture covering

Texture finish can be removed if you should want to get rid of it at some future date. Since this is a messy job, before you begin, remove all the furniture and cover the floor with plastic sheeting.

The easiest way is to use a texture paint remover. Apply with a brush and leave to penetrate for at least 30 minutes. When softened, strip off with a stripping knife. Then wash with water and washing-up liquid before redecorating. Always wear protective gloves and goggles when using any caustic chemicals and keep children and pets well away.

Another option is to use a steam wallpaper stripper. The steam seeps into the coating which can then be removed with a stripping knife. Never sand a texture coating, as some used to contain asbestos which should not be inhaled.

Tortoiseshelling

The tortoiseshell effect is an illusion-istic paint technique, designed to imitate the wonderful markings and marbled shades of real tortoiseshell. It was the shell of the sea turtle which was first used in the East as an inlay or veneer on small items of furniture. As tortoise-shell decoration became more popular in the West from the 17th century onwards, it was imitated by craftsmen in the making of picture frames, cabinets and tables. When the sea turtle was officially declared an endangered species in 1973, the paint effect became an ecologically sound, as well as a less expensive, substitute for the real thing.

If you want to produce a very close imitation, you should go for a small painting project as real tortoiseshell was only used in small pieces because of its scarcity. Hairbrushes, trays, wooden panels and picture frames look particu-larly effective. However, more ambi-tious projects, such as an entire wall or tabletop, can look sensational. With these the paint finish is generally applied with less detail. This looks less realistic, but takes on a beautiful fantasy finish of its own.

Real tortoiseshell varies in pattern. It can look blotchy, like leopard skin, or more stripy, or it can have hardly any definite markings at all. Colour is variable too; some tortoiseshell is very light with dark brown and black mark-ings on a tawny background. Other examples are of a darker, reddish colour.

To create a tortoiseshell effect layers of tinted glaze are built up. It is important that this glaze stays wet as you add each extra layer, so that you can use a brush to blend the colours together. Although the glaze will take 24 hours to dry completely, it becomes unworkable after about 30 minutes. This time may be extended slightly with the addition of a little white spirit or linseed oil, but it will still be necessary to work quickly if you are painting a large area like a table, or a panelled door. To get the feel of the process begin with a smaller project – a picture frame would be ideal.

▶ *Panel power*
A plain wooden door can be made into a exciting focal point with the addition of painted tortoiseshell panels. Here the glowing russet coloured panels stand out well as the frame is painted in a plain but complementary colour.

Painting a tortoiseshell door

For a convincing tortoiseshell effect, it is well worth practising on an old piece of wood before starting on the real thing. When you are ready to paint the door itself, it is probably best to paint the tortoiseshell panels first as the overall colour may end up slightly different from the one you expected. This won't matter if you match the door frame colour to it afterwards.

Preparing the door

Polished door panels should be stripped using white spirit and wire wool, then washed down with a mild detergent solution. Use paint stripper to remove any old paint. The bare wood should then be sanded down and primed.

Mixing the glaze

To make 300ml (½ pint): squeeze 15cm (6in) raw sienna oil colour from a 22ml tube into a jar. Thin with 60ml (2fl oz) white spirit and add 240ml (8fl oz) glaze.

Softening brush

paint brush

small sable brush

hog's hair fitch

TORTOISESHELL PANELS

Materials

Panelled door to be painted
Basecoat Use buff eggshell paint.
Scumble glaze
White spirit
Artist's oil colours in raw sienna, burnt sienna and burnt umber.
Brushes: To produce the tortoiseshell effect, you need to use special brushes: an **ordinary paint brush** for applying the base coat, a **hog's hair fitch** for applying the coloured glaze, a **softening brush** for blending and softening the colours and a **small sable brush** for spattering paint and white spirit.
Lint-free cloth to soften 'dragged' lines in the glaze
Clear polyurethane varnish to protect the finished panels

1 Applying the basecoat Using an ordinary paint brush, give each panel two coats of eggshell, sanding down lightly in between each coat and carefully wiping away any dust.

▲ **Turning turtle** Here a spectacular effect is achieved by using an enlarged tortoiseshell pattern over the walls as well as on the door. The novelty value of such fantastic decoration is probably well worth the effort.

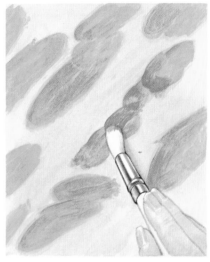

2 Painting on the tinted glaze
Using the paint brush, apply a coat of the mixed glaze over the panels, one after the other. Work the brush backwards and forwards, making diagonal strokes across each one. If you end up with a dragged effect, you should go back over the panel and soften the lines by dabbing gently with a lint-free cloth.

3 Creating the markings Add a little raw sienna to the basic glaze to darken it. Using the fitch in small diagonal strokes, paint in some rough-edged cloudlike patches. Paint patches of different sizes, the largest of which should be about 7cm (2¾in) in length. Space the patches quite unevenly and make some of them overlap each other.

4 Adding a reddish tint Mix a little burnt sienna with the glaze and add some small patches using the fitch to paint diagonally as before. Paint some between the larger patches, some inside and some just overlapping them. Burnt sienna is a strong colour so be sparing with it or it will swamp every other shade. Use more for a very red effect.

5 Darkening the patches Darken the glaze again by mixing in some burnt umber. Now make some darker strokes mainly in the centre of the larger raw sienna patches. Add more burnt umber to the glaze and make smaller marks in the centre of the previous burnt umber strokes.

6 Softening the colour outlines Using the softening brush, blur the colour outlines by brushing over each panel with light strokes back and forth in the same diagonal direction as the patches were painted. Repeat this process until you are satisfied with the colours.

7 Adding depth of colour Use a fine sable or mock-sable paint brush to paint in a few tiny spots of pure burnt umber. Alternatively spatter dark glaze over each panel.

To spatter colour, dip the tip of the paint brush into the glaze, then tap the brush handle smartly against a straight edge held over the panel. Now use the softening brush again, to lightly merge the resulting burnt umber spots into the rest of the tortoiseshell pattern.

8 Protecting the surface Once the glaze has dried, apply a coat of gloss varnish to give a gleaming polished look. When dry, rub this down with fine glasspaper and wipe down before applying another two coats of varnish for protection and a really deep shine.

tip

Antiquing the finish
This can be done by spattering some white spirit over some or all the panels immediately after spattering the glaze. Allow 30 seconds for the white spirit to take effect before using the softening brush.

Larger projects

While small objects look best painted in a detailed way, it is often more visually pleasing to take a different approach when painting over a large flat surface such as a table or a wall.

One possibility is to simply enlarge the patched pattern described in the instructions on pages 54–55. Another way is to create a gentler, less detailed finish over the whole surface by extra softening and merging of the colours.

Another variation is to create the tortoiseshell effect in unusual colour combinations. Various shades of red, blue or green can look dramatic over large surfaces where you are generally less likely to be trying to produce a very close imitation of the real thing.

▲ Photo finish
The table illustrated has been given quite a light, tawny tortoiseshell finish, achieved by a sparing use of the Burnt Sienna and Raw Umber oil colours.

The diagonal brushwork can be clearly seen over the whole surface although extra, more random softening strokes have been added after the first diagonal ones. This creates an original, uncluttered and carefree effect, which is particularly well suited to a modern style of interior decoration.

▶ Patching it up
Although extremely time consuming, it can be very rewarding to work in detail over a really large area.

In the traditional country reception room illustrated, an elaborate tortoiseshell effect has been used to create a striking visual feature of the cornice and the architrave around both the doors.

The speckled look has been achieved by painting a lot of overlapping patches and spattered spots in contrasting colours (Burnt Sienna and Black), without merging or softening the lines between them.

Vinegar graining

This colourful, bold and decorative finish was popular in the 19th century. It was quick to produce and used extensively by early American country craftsmen exploiting cheap and widely available materials. The rich colours and striking patterns have a rustic appeal that has made it more popular with many people than the painted wood graining from which it was originally derived.

Unlike wood graining, which sets out to deceive the eye by mimicking the grain patterns and tones of a particular timber, vinegar graining uses purely decorative colours such as wine red, sea blue or forest green over a white basecoat or a paler tone of the top colour. A dark colour on a light background shows up the patterns best.

The topcoat, or glaze, is a sticky mixture of vinegar or beer and powder paint. While the paint is still tacky, a wide range of materials can be rolled or dabbed on to it to create decorative designs. Some of the most frequently used pattern makers are putty, leaves, feathers, combs and rags. Even thumb prints add to the decoration.

This bold finish is best applied to flat surfaces. Small items like trays, boxes, plant stands and table tops are all suitable. The finish looks especially effective, however, on larger pieces such as a chest of drawers, blanket chest, cupboard doors or a wardrobe. For large panels and flat surfaces use bold patterns; save the subtle effects for small items, frameworks and mouldings.

Materials

Oil-based paint A matt finish is required for the base coat. White undercoat, used normally under gloss paint on skirtings and doors, is ideal. If you want a pastel colour base you can use eggshell or tint leftover undercoat with artists' oil paints.

Powder paint To colour the glaze you need to use powder paint. Choose from children's powder paint or artists' powdered pigment.

To give the glaze the necessary sticky

▲ A treasure of a chest
The combing and rolling of the mellow glaze on this wooden trunk gently accentuates its genuine antiquity.

quality and provide the bold patterns, you also need **malt vinegar** and **sugar** together with **washing-up liquid**. Stale ale could be used instead of vinegar.

Varnish As the paint used for forming the patterns is water based it is not permanent. For a tough finish you will need to use two or three coats of clear polyurethane wood varnish in a satin or gloss finish.

You will also need a couple of **pots** for mixing paint, **teaspoons**, two 2-5cm (¾-2in) **paint brushes** for applying the glaze and the varnish. **Rubber gloves** will prevent your hands getting messy when you are making the pattern. **Glasspaper** will take off any old finish and smooth the surface between coats of varnish. Use **wet-and-dry paper** to remove any sheen on a newly-prepared surface.

▼ **Naturally impressive**
Look for pattern makers everywhere;
commonplace objects and foliage
leave fascinating imprints in the
glaze.

Pattern-making equipment

Putty or Plasticine can be shaped into short sausages for rolling across the surface. Use it like a rolling-pin to create a decorative rope pattern. Roll on a second curving line next to the first for a coiled rope effect. Form patterns by dabbing small coils of modelling material on to the surface.

Feathers and leaves pressed on to the surface come away leaving an imprint of their natural outline. Bunches of pine needles dragged through the glaze create a wispy, swirling effect. The Americans used dried corn cobs in the same way.

Paper folded concertina style, then held like a fan and pressed on the surface makes a good design for a corner.

A comb run through the glaze gives a series of fine parallel lines. Cross these for a woven texture. An Afro comb is an excellent tool for this purpose.

A bunched rag or crumpled paper removes just a little of the top colour to give a subtle pattern. Experiment with a crumpled plastic bag as well.

Thumb and finger prints provide a signature mark that cannot be forged. The top of a cork can be used in a similar way. Try out any other household objects you think may have pattern-making potential.

VINEGAR GRAINING

1 Preparing the surface The item to be decorated needs to have a smooth, grease-free surface. A painted finish in good condition can simply be sanded with fine glasspaper to key the surface. A varnished or polished surface will need to be completely removed with medium and fine glasspaper. Then give one coat of primer and two coats of undercoat, or one of undercoat and one of eggshell finish. Allow the final coat to dry well, then rub down with wet-and-dry paper and soapy water, to remove any sheen, and wipe dry.

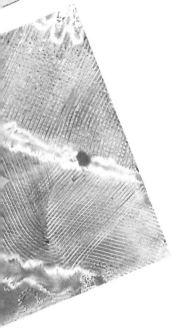

2 Mixing the glaze Into a jar pour 125ml (4fl oz) vinegar or beer. Add a teaspoonful of sugar and a teaspoon of washing-up liquid and mix well. In a bowl put two teaspoons of powder paint and mix thoroughly with a little of the vinegar/beer solution to form a paste. Add more liquid until the mixture is the consistency of single cream.

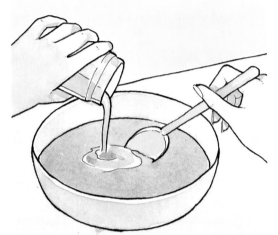

3 Checking the glaze Using a paintbrush, paint a couple of sheets of paper with the glaze, then coat the first surface to be decorated. Leave the paint to become tacky. It should take about 8-10 minutes.

Test if the glaze is ready by rolling a small sausage of putty or Plasticine over one of the glaze-coated sheets of paper. A glaze that is still too wet will flow back and obliterate the design. If it is too wet, wait a further minute or two. Then experiment again on the second sheet of paper. A glaze that has dried too much becomes difficult to work with and will not accept the pattern. If it is too dry wipe the glaze off with a damp cloth and re-coat the surface.

4 Creating the design When the glaze is ready, use your chosen materials to form a pattern on the first surface of the object you are decorating. Once you are happy with the design, leave it to dry for about an hour. If you make a mistake, wipe the glaze off and start again.

Repeat for any other surfaces. It is best to decorate each surface individually because the glaze dries quickly.

5 Protecting the finish When it is dry, the paint loses its sheen but this is restored by varnishing. Apply 2 or 3 coats of clear polyurethane wood varnish. Allow it to dry between coats and rub down lightly with fine grade glasspaper before applying the next one.

▲▶ Taken from nature
*Ivy leaves and fronds of yew have
been used to print a bold design on
the tray shown above.*

*The table shown right is
decorated using various techniques
– rolled putty on the top, pine
needles on the narrow stretcher bars
and crumpled paper on the lower
part of the legs.*

tip

Planning your design
Check your choice of colours
on a piece of paper first. Then
experiment with the pattern-
making materials. When you
have decided which effect you
like best, you are ready to
recreate your planned design
on the item you are decorating.